Escape the LIFE TRAP

THE GUIDE TO BECOMING THE ULTIMATE VERSION OF YOURSELF AND LIVING YOUR BEST LIFE!

By Ben Hulme

WWW.ESCAPETHELIFETRAP.COM

Index

For my daughters.

1.

- Mission -

I knew there was a reason I got in that Lamborghini, but I didn't ever think it was to break my neck. In that crash, in that moment, my life changed. Dramatically.

My story has already inspired thousands and my mission now is to motivate and inspire over a million people. I want my story to be the catalyst that enables you to start living your dreams now, whilst you are still looking forward to your future, rather than looking back at your past with regret.

Please don't regret the life you live by doing yourself the injustice of discovering you've done too little too late. Use this book as the boost to you getting what you want out of your life, because no matter what people say, this really isn't a dress rehearsal!

I am tired of hearing people saying 'something will turn up', because it won't! You need to be the force that changes your future because you are the only one standing in the way of your success.

Don't get caught in what I call the life trap, drifting from weekend to weekend. Make your life count, be someone, achieve your goals and dreams. Don't wait for a life-changing incident to be the moment you realise what you're missing, leverage my near-death experience and start being the best you, NOW!

Ben Hulme

BenHulme.com
TheBootCamper.com

2.

- The second life -

"We all have two lives. The second one starts when we realise that we only have one."

- Tom Hiddleston

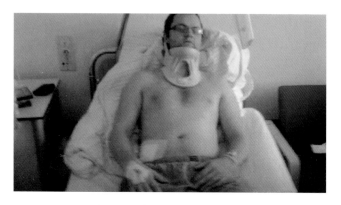

- In hospital after my 6 hour operation -

- The wrecked Lamborghini Murcielago I was a passenger in -

This book isn't about me. It's about YOU and improving your life. But first I need to share a bit of my story so that you understand where I'm coming from and why I have written this book to help you.

It all started when I woke up from a 6-hour operation in a random hospital in Germany. I was dazed and confused, not knowing exactly where I was. It was strange, scary and surreal. But that was the defining moment, the start of my new life. That was the 'pinch yourself moment' that no one ever forgets.

I had broken and dislocated my neck in a car accident when the driver of the Lamborghini I was in lost control at high speed and crashed into a tree. What a nightmare... It really wasn't pretty. The car was a wreck and so was I (FYI the driver walked away unhurt).

Before the operation the doctor asked me (a rather high on morphine 25-year-old) to sign a document in German (a language I can't speak!). I was scared. I was in a foreign country with a broken neck unsure of what the hell this doctor was getting me to sign. In his rather broken English he explained that I had to sign my agreement to a surgery that came with some rather 'interesting' outcomes.

- **A 1 in 3 chance I would be paralysed from the neck down.**
- **A 1 in 3 chance I would die.**
- **A 1 in 3 chance I would survive, but would most likely have arthritis in my neck.**

This was scary. The fact I could either die or be paralysed from the neck down was all I could focus on. I freaked out. What had I done to myself? What had I done to my family and friends?

How were they going to deal with this if I died or if I was paralysed from the neck down and needed to have full-time care?

I had no choice, I had to sign this document because the operation was essential. I needed the operation immediately.

I signed.

The operation involved taking some bone from my hip to be placed in my neck behind a metal plate and four pins that were used to fuse together C3 and C4. The surgeons would also have to remove some broken bone fragments that were close to touching my spinal column which, if left in my neck, could eventually paralyse or kill me. They would also need to re-align the dislocated vertebrae. On top of that they would be opening up my neck from the front and I would have a big scar to show for it. Would I ever look the same again? Would I be ugly with a huge scar on my neck? There was so much going through my head, I was in a really bad place.

My brother happened to be in Germany at the same time as my accident and he rushed to the hospital upon receiving the news, getting there just before I went into surgery. I am sure he remembers it well, it was an emotional moment for both of us.

The doctor called my parents back in the UK, who had already been informed of the accident, so that I could tell them I loved them and that I hoped to see them on the other side. I didn't tell them what the odds of me surviving were, but needless to say, it was an emotional call. I remember just choking up and not being able to talk at all,

I literally couldn't get a word out. I was in floods of tears and could hardly contain myself. They knew what I was trying to say but they just felt so helpless that they were in another country whilst their eldest son was about to go under the knife.

I went into the operating theatre staring at the hospital ceiling thinking that this was the last thing I would ever see. The doctor injected the anesthetic and I remember being told to count to ten.

When I woke up my brother was by my hospital bed. It was the best sight ever. I was alive and had a familiar face to tell me all went well.

I was in hospital for the next 8 days and I don't think I could have got through it without my brother being there as I literally couldn't move. I had to eat hospital food, which is terrible in Germany (Sorry! But have you tried sauerkraut soup?). I couldn't swallow properly so it was a liquid diet for me. Soups and yogurts were about all I could get down. No offense to the Germans but they aren't known for their cuisine, however they are known for being fantastic engineers so I believe that I was in one of the best places in the world for an operation like this, but the food really sucked!

From the first day of my 'new life' I had many questions going around in my head that I will never forget. If I had died in that accident:

- **Was my life the best it could have been?**
- **Was I the best person I could be?**
- **Had I achieved my dreams and ambitions?**
- **Would I have left a legacy?**

The problem was that the answer to all my burning questions was: 'NO'.

If I had died in that accident or during the operation I can safely say with 100% sincerity that I would NOT have been happy with who I was or what I had achieved. I had great plans that I wanted to accomplish but I kept putting them off and had I died I would have never achieved them. I was just drifting through life, not knowing how quickly it could be taken away from me. I was caught in what I call the "life trap".

Don't get me wrong, I had a great life before the accident, but my life seemed to revolve around what others thought I should be doing. I was basically a sheep following the routine and formalities set out by the society we live in.

Like many young people today, the reality is that I ended up living for the weekend. The thing I enjoyed the most was partying with my friends, drinking and without putting too much of a blunt point on it, chasing girls! Of course they were good times (I could tell you stories but that's for another day) and I have some very fond memories that I will never forget and a few that I would rather forget!

But...

Looking back now, I had caught myself in the 'life trap', which I will go into detail about during this book. I was just drifting through life one weekend at a time. Of course I had dreams and ambitions (who doesn't?) I had not actually thought about life seriously enough to achieve them. I was young, single and carefree, thinking that one day something would turn up. Of course something did turn up, and it nearly killed me.

I wasn't living up to my true potential. I wasn't being the best version of me. If I had died in that car accident I would have left nothing. Literally nothing.

This couldn't carry on. Not in my second life. Why would I want to do that when I had been given this beautiful gift?

And that's when it happened. In my hospital bed in Germany after my near-death experience, I realised that I had to make this life count and help others get out of the life trap (regardless of whether they knew they were in it or not).

In this book you will discover that YOU are potentially caught in the life trap. You need to wake up and stop drifting through your life, living for the weekend, or living a life of routine and boredom stuck in a dead-end job or a lifestyle that you hate. My goal in this book is to awaken you to the opportunities available to you to live a meaningful life of happiness and abundance so that every day feels like a weekend – dare I say it, even a Monday! I want to help you live your dreams. It may seem obvious when I say it, but I want you to realise that this is your one and only chance to live the best life you can. Laugh more, smile more, be happy and live a fulfilled life that you can look back at and be proud of.

I want you to leverage my near-death experience for yourself and realise that you might not get a second chance like I did. You never know when your life will be taken away from you and it's shocking how fast it can go. I never thought I would come that close to dying and it scares the hell out of me thinking about what the outcome could have been.

Of course, I hope you live a long, healthy life of abundance but chances are that if you don't snap out of the life trap then it may not happen and you may look back from your deathbed with regret. How much would that suck?

You really need to act now to change your future. This book highlights some strategies and techniques that could really benefit you now and in your future.

I often get asked if I regret getting in that Lamborghini. And to tell you the truth... I believe with my entire soul that I was supposed to be in that car accident. I believe that I was in there for a reason and that reason is to help and inspire others to live the best lives they can.

Sounds crazy right?

When I got back to the UK I went to see a neurosurgeon and upon analysing my X-rays he said, 'Ben I have seen people paralysed or dead from lesser injuries than yours. It's genuinely a miracle that you are still alive, it's crucial that you now make something of your second chance at life.'

This was powerful for me to hear and something that I will never forget. I am truly happy and grateful that it happened because I learnt a valuable lesson that I am now able to share with you. I hope that this will be the catalyst to change your life without having to go through all the pain and suffering that I experienced. You can achieve the success you want, and you need to be aware that you are the only one standing in the way of that success.

The actual physical and mental side of breaking your neck and then the recovery process is really bad. I wouldn't wish it upon anyone. It's terribly painful and very unpleasant. My recovery took 2 years in total, but I still have some side effects from the accident and there is a 75% chance I'll get arthritis in my neck when I'm older. But I see the positive in everything, I am truly blessed to be here and to convey this message to help others.

I took my recovery slowly and made sure that I did everything the doctors, the neurosurgeons and the physiotherapists told me to do. The thing that took the most time was my mental recovery. I found it very hard to regain the confidence to be a passenger in a car again. During my recovery I had vivid nightmares where I kept being killed in horrific ways. I won't go into it as I don't want to open those doors again, but needless to say, I ended up seeing a counsellor who took me through a fantastic hypnotherapy course that really helped with my PTSD. I would say that I've now made a 95% recovery physically, but my life has changed dramatically because of this journey and, to be honest, my mindset is 10 times better than what it was. I've become unstoppable, with a thirst for achieving my dreams and pushing myself beyond what I ever thought I could achieve.

I want you to have this unstoppable mindset and in this book you will discover the exact strategies I use so that you can make your dreams a reality for yourself – no matter what they are.

During my recovery, I learned that time really is the most precious thing and the most incredible healer. Time is on our side, to be used as a tool to achieve results (more about this later in the book). I am a much better person from this experience but I am not the same person I was. I am proud of who I have become and I am always striving every day to be the best version of me. I will never stop.

Escape the LIFE TRAP

This is a guide about becoming the best you, to becoming more confident and to living a fulfilled life of health, wealth and happiness. This is a book about taking positive steps towards your success every day. By applying the advice and strategies found within the following chapters you can fully expect to improve any aspect of your life very quickly, almost instantly.

I got out of the life trap but I learnt the hard way. Now it's time for you to do the same and start living your best life. Start achieving your goals, dreams and ambitions. Let's do it!

3.

- Hard truths you need to hear -

This chapter might not sit well with some but if you truly want the successful future you dream of then you need to hear this from someone, and it might as well be me.

This chapter seemed like a natural starting point. You now know part of my story, the car accident part anyway (more to follow) but you now need to hear some hard truths to open your eyes as to why and how you need to change your future. NOW.

So let's get into it...

1. Don't be a 'Phone Zombie'

Too many people spend nearly all their time browsing their smartphones and iPads to get the latest videos, photos and news from social media. This has become an epidemic that's taking over our planet and the human race. It's a zombie virus and it's getting worse. I call it the 'Phone Zombie'. Just lift your head from the screen next time you are in public and watch the number of people who are face down in their phones.

We are all guilty of it but the fact is that this is not healthy. Hands up, I use my phone a lot, but I use it for building my businesses not for procrastinating and wasting time. There is a HUGE difference. Let me explain why the Phone Zombie virus is going to get you nowhere, fast...

The data that's being taken in by you as a Phone Zombie IS NOT breaking news. It's just 'fluff' taking up headspace and satisfying your desire (potentially unknown desire) to be 'kept in the loop' but on a global scale. This has become a HABIT. One you need to break - FAST!

Social-media browsing can of course be interesting but most of it will be highly irrelevant news that someone has literally broadcast over the Internet. It's most likely a negative comment or post, a moan about someone's life, a meme, a short video or a photo of someone's lunch!

The problem is that you are cluttering up your brain with ridiculous chatter that is coming from your peer group, celebrities or even friends of friends. There is simply no need to pay attention to this data all the time. It goes in, takes up your time and then has zero impact on your life, except to waste your time. Time which you will never get back.

This fluff has no meaningful purpose to your life. Seriously. Listen. If you have to browse Facebook and can't be without it, do yourself a favour and put a stopwatch or a countdown timer on (yes your phone has that too) and cap your social-media browsing to 10 minutes every 6 hours. Trust me, you won't miss anything, it will still be on your newsfeed and you will get a lot more out of your day. If something is really, crucially urgent, someone will contact you directly, so everything else is just noise.

That's the reality of it. Important news isn't broadcast on Facebook so stop filling your head and your time with it. You have to be so careful what you put into your brain and where you spend your time if you really want to be the best you can be. More about time management later, but start thinking about how you spend your time because if you become a Phone Zombie you won't get that time back. Ever. It's a disease and if you let the addiction set in you won't even notice that you're doing it, but many people around you will. I see this often.

Recently I was in a restaurant and a family walked in. I'm going to detail how their meal went. (Yes, I was analysing their behaviour and should have been minding my own business but their situation isn't uncommon and I've seen it many times before. Maybe you have too or perhaps you are guilty of it?)

This young family sat down in the restaurant and ordered their drinks. I would say the parents were in their late twenties and had two young children with them. They immediately got their phones out and started browsing Facebook like zombies. I knew it was Facebook as I could see pretty clearly and I'd recognise that upwards thumb flick anywhere! Their children were playing games on their iPads. Everyone had their face buried in a screen. When the waitress came back over with their drinks the first thing they then asked for was the WiFi code so they could get online without using their cellular data (why would you want to spend money on being anti-social?!).

This bugs me big time. Don't get me wrong, there is a time and place for iPads. I am a full-time single father to two daughters and believe me, sometimes they go on their tablets, but 95% of the time we relax, chat and enjoy a nice meal or we go 'old school' and I take colouring books and pencils for the girls.

I also run businesses that require me to be online a fair bit. But when it's a meal time and the girls and I have made the effort to go out, the phone gets switched off or it goes in my pocket. Family time, socialising with friends or work colleagues should be about exactly that, spending time with people you want to spend time with! Not looking at the forehead of the person sitting in front of you throughout the meal whilst being a Phone Zombie.

Anyway, back to the point. This young family hardly said a word to each other throughout the whole meal. The parents just chuckled away to themselves when they saw something funny on their Facebook. In fact, I think they said more to their friends via instant messenger than they did to each other verbally the entire meal! The kids were zombies, focussed on their screens, so much so that none of them realised that their food had arrived.

I know I shouldn't be so nosey, but the thing is, this isn't an isolated incident. I saw the same family again the next week at the same restaurant doing exactly the same thing. The sad reality is that this is happening right now in every restaurant, in every cafe and in every living room in every place all over the world.

You know exactly what I'm talking about, don't you? Of course you do because you do it. I do, we all do, it's become part of our lives now. But it's those of us who make a conscious effort to restrict the time we are Phone Zombies who will ultimately get further in life and have:

A) Better memories
B) Better experiences with friends and loved ones
C) Greater success

People worry about their computers getting a virus but it's your brain that's got the virus from the computer, tablet or mobile device. Oh the irony!

Computers have given us the virus and it's killing people's futures by literally stealing their time. When you are next in a restaurant or in a public place, look around and you will see what I'm talking about. Social media has changed the world in so many positive ways. But there are so many negative changes that have come about too, some of which I think have become a real drain on society and human interaction. It's a shame.

If you want to really get far in your life, reach your goals and realise your dreams, eliminate the Phone Zombie virus from your brain now. You don't need it. Appreciate what's going on around you, not what's going on inside your phone. It's just fluff and it can wait. Any news that is actually important will get to you when the time is right.

Of course if you use your phone a lot for work you will need to be checking and writing emails, and potentially some social media, and that is absolutely fine, everything in moderation. But unless it's taking your life forward – for example, making you money – then you really should consider limiting your social-media intake to 10 minutes every 6 hours. Maximum. Try it. It's not easy at first but you'll thank me later for all the extra time you have on your hands.

2. The world doesn't owe you anything

You are alive. That is a gift. You can do whatever you want to do with your life. You can choose to screw it up and waste it or you can choose to make something of it, be someone, achieve your goals and really see the true success you desire.

The important thing to note here is that this choice is yours and only yours.

You do however have to understand something: The world doesn't owe you anything. Literally nothing except for death. Death is the 'ying' to the 'yang' of life. As obvious as it is, we are all born and we will all die. Fact. But I really think some people forget that fact and just drift through their life without giving it much thought. Whether there is another life after death is a healthy debate but let's assume for the benefit of this book that there isn't. You have one chance to make your time on this spinning rock the best it can be. What you do in between life and death is completely up to you.

You need to awaken yourself to the fact that this is your one-and-only chance to shine. Use it to push forward every day to achieve the success and greatness you truly deserve.

Please don't leave it to chance because it won't happen. Don't be a drifter saying, 'It'll work itself out' or, 'Something will turn up' – because it won't. Do yourself a favour and don't fall for the dreaded life trap.

The world doesn't owe you a thing so you need to be sure that you're prepared to put time and dedication into moving forward to where you want to ultimately end up. It's there for the taking and can be achieved, but only you can make it happen and that starts today.

You have to work your backside off in all aspects of your life. No one ever got anywhere in life by being lazy so be prepared to put the effort into your future now while you have the time and energy, before you get too old and regret not doing more when you were able to (although it's never too late).

Becoming successful in anything ultimately takes time, patience and determination. They say it takes 10,000 hours to become an expert in anything but by understanding that the world doesn't owe you a thing you are able to make the subtle shift from expecting something to just 'turn up' to an awareness that what you achieve is a direct result of the effort you put in. Are you willing to put in the 10,000 hours to get your life where you want it to be? You should be, as no one else will.

But it's crucial to know that the effort doesn't have to be a chore. If you're working towards what you really desire and what you really want then every day should be a real blessing. Every day should be a joy because you're working towards your dreams and doing what you love. Anything is possible. How big are your dreams and how badly do you want to achieve them? You decide.

3. You can never quit. Literally never.
Quitting is not the same as failing. We all fail. It's how we learn and move forward towards perfection. I will explain more about failure later in the book, but basically failing is when you tried something and it didn't work out. This is also called 'research', so by trying to make this 'thing' work, you will have learned something that will take you forward in the future. This isn't bad, it's actually a very good thing and shouldn't be seen as a negative.

Failing is entirely different to quitting because if you truly have dreams and goals then you won't be able to quit. You can try to quit. You can say 'enough is enough' and accept defeat and 'quit' but time is the best healer and you will end up wanting to try again. It's in your DNA. You will always have a thirst for that dream, that goal, that ambition.

If you truly want something, quitting is impossible because you will soon be back on that mission. What your heart desires the body and brain will work towards. Therefore it is impossible to really quit and why would you want to, anyway? Once you realise that failure isn't a bad thing it all becomes a journey. A journey where doors and avenues open to take you to the success that you desire.

4. You will have naysayers

"If you're absent during my struggle, don't expect to be present during my success." – *Will Smith*

This is a tricky topic for me to write about as I've had a tough experience with so called 'naysayers' in the past. It's most likely that it will happen to you too.

Keep your eye out for people holding you back because it's not always as blatantly obvious as you might first think. The naysayers can be in disguise as friends and believe it or not, even family. Sometimes it can even be your partner or spouse. Most of the time these people don't even know they are holding you back. It's not intentional, it's just the way they have been educated or the fact that they assume you won't make it and don't want to pick up the pieces when you get hurt.

But more often than not people are sneaky, they will intentionally try to hold you back and I can almost guarantee that this will happen to you. It is a very sad reality of the human race and happens all the time, and will undoubtedly become part of your journey.

By going after your dreams and ambitions you are showing weaknesses in other people's lives and many won't like that. That's their choice. They are on their own journey so don't worry about what they say. Most likely they don't have what it takes to push for their dreams. But do step back and start to notice who the people are who justify their own life situation when you tell them your goals and dreams.

They tend to be the people who haven't fulfilled their dreams or achieved their goals yet. Or those who have actually given up totally and pretend they are happy.

Trust me when I say that the biggest jeers come from the cheapest seats! Think about that for a second.

By saying that you have dreams and goals and that you are going after them, you will highlight others' weaknesses. Subsequently they will try to 'subtly' pull you down and hold you back by telling you why you're making a mistake, that you're taking too big a risk, you're looking foolish, you're embarrassing yourself, you're being selfish, you will fail etc. You will start to notice these trends in their attitude towards you every time you're talking about your goals and dreams.

This type of behaviour will usually be from people you least expect. Often it can be family, even close family, who hold you back. They will say, 'It's because I love you and don't want to see you get hurt when/if you fail' or 'What about the mortgage?' or 'I love you and think you should be realistic with your expectations', and they will definitely say, 'Don't get your hopes up'. (I hate that expression!) DEFINITELY do get your hopes up, please do, because it's important.

Of course it's nice to know these people love you and don't want to see you get hurt but their naysaying is actually having the opposite effect of love and it is not allowing you to be free. Free to put your full effort into achieving your dreams which will ultimately benefit your family and friends in the long term anyway!). Sometimes you will feel that you want to move forward and chase your dreams but the safety, security and warmth of your family tells you different. This is normal, you have spent the most fragile early years of your life listening to advice from your family so you are naturally programmed to listen and do what they say and advise. Think carefully about whose advice you take. This is your life, remember, no one else's.

Things like 'look both ways when you cross the road', 'don't talk to strangers' and 'be careful when you go out' are common expressions we have all heard from people we love, trust and respect. Often from our parents. We have an instant 'safety' association with the people who gave us this advice when we were young and it's hard to disregard advice about your future from people who have had your back from day one. But sometimes it's necessary to make your own path, because the reality is that often the people who love you will want you to stay within their comfort zone, within their control.

Your comfort zone and the comfort zone of others will be very different. To achieve the success you crave, you will need to push your boundaries, which is something many are not willing to do themselves. It is too much of a risk for them so they will try to lay their lack of self-belief on you. In reality, life is a risk because you will never get out alive; so take full advantage and push your boundaries. You never know what you are capable of until you really try.

You must always think about who you take advice from. Some people will totally 'dig' what you're doing and support you without even thinking twice. Many will tell you that it's hard work but to give it your best shot. And others will simply tell you that you can't do it and that you're mad to pursue that direction, that dream, that goal... But remember: this is your life, so listen to your gut instinct. Naysayers will always stay within their comfort zone or stick to so called 'safer' options, saying things such as, 'Why do you want to do that and take that risk when you could go and get a job?'. Which, by the way, is a question to answer. If you took the 'safer' option and took the job then you have to question if you are really living your passion and being true to yourself. You could potentially regret it later because, as I said before, time won't allow you to give up on your dreams and the urge to try again will come back. Except this time it'll be 5 years down the line and you will be kicking yourself for not doing it sooner. Now you will be kicking yourself for taking advice from that family member who was so 'qualified' to give you that life lesson! I repeat, think carefully about who you take advice from. This is your life, remember, not theirs.

You need to be chasing your dreams now, even if that means working on your ambitions alongside a day job, working evenings and weekends. You must never stop chasing your life purpose because of what someone else has told you they think is right for you.

Luckily, I have a very supportive family and I'm grateful to them every day because they have supported me through my successes, my failures, the high times and the low times and that means the world to me. Of course there were others who just didn't 'get me'. They didn't understand what I was trying to achieve and offered their (unwanted) advice and yet they are the ones still broadcasting on Facebook to all the Phone Zombies that they hate Mondays with a hashtag like #FML. They are stuck in the life trap and I doubt any of them will ever get out. Sorry guys, I tried, you just didn't listen! But some people, perhaps you, don't have supportive friends and family and that needs to be addressed. I'm not telling you to go and tell everyone your grand plan about how you're going to smash life, live the dream and become a superstar.

Personally I would advise keeping some things a little closer to your chest by only telling those you know will support you (but know how to handle it if they don't). Most people have been conditioned to think that's not actually possible and they won't understand it because that's something only the 'lucky' people do. WRONG! That's what happens to people who believe in themselves and work their backsides off every day until they get to where they want to be.

You will need some support but as you move forward you are going to notice changes in people. Some might not like what you are doing, who you are becoming and what you are trying and going to achieve. They might mock you and tell you to 'be realistic' because you are highlighting weaknesses in their character and they don't feel comfortable with that.

So please tread carefully regarding who you talk to about your dreams and ambitions, and watch closely how people react when you start going in a different direction. Watch how they react when you start losing weight, making more money, getting some media coverage, learning a new skill, developing as an individual, smiling more. You will quickly learn who your real friends are. Trust me, I have lost many so-called friends over many events in my life and you know what? I am better off without them. To quote the legend Will Smith: 'If you're absent during my struggle, don't expect to be present during my success.'

You will certainly have to make some tough choices along the way, I guarantee it. You don't want naysayers holding you back with their little comments and snide remarks about you moving forward with your life. If they are not 100% behind you, even if they are neutral, you don't need them. They are not true friends to you and you should think carefully about how you proceed with that relationship. Do you want to be hanging out with people who just hold you back because of their limiting beliefs? Or do you want to blossom and grow with a peer group who are on the same road to success? I know which I would choose every single time.

I choose to hang out with people who are going places. People who take their health seriously, people who run successful businesses, people who talk about real life rather than just reality TV and soap operas, people who don't spend every weekend partying and getting drunk, people who don't waste their time being a Phone Zombie, people who don't read newspapers and the tabloids from cover to cover filling their head with propaganda and negativity every day. Motivational speaker Jim Rohn once said that you are the average of the 5 people you spend the most time with. So choose wisely, my friend, your future depends on it.

Of course, I am not saying completely ditch all your friends who don't understand what you're trying to do. You must respect their opinion but do what you want anyway. I repeat, this is your life not theirs. All I am saying is be careful about who you take advice from. If you want to know what's wrong with your car you don't take it to a dentist to get it fixed. If you have something wrong with your teeth you don't go to the mechanic. It's the same with success. You don't go to someone who's unsuccessful to find out how to succeed, you go to someone who's where you want to be.

When I was at school I really got into playing squash. It was brilliant and I started as a complete beginner - but I received some very good advice from my coach and that advice stuck with me for many years for many different parts of my life. He told me that if you want to improve at squash, you must not play against the same person all the time; play against people who are better than you, people with more experience, until you beat them and then move to the next person until you beat them etc. This is the best way to move forward and improve

I remembered this lesson because it became very apparent when I got to the position of number 2 seed in my school from a complete beginner. I then played the number 1 player from our school but he genuinely was at another level. By the time I started to get competitive with him my time at school was up, I was 18 and ready for the next chapter in my life, but I learnt to always push myself to be better by learning from those who are doing better than me. This is generally true for any area of life that you want to improve.

Don't get caught out by taking advice from people who are not where you want to be. Unwanted opinions will be everywhere but let your success do the talking. Be the inspiration they need in their lives by showing them that dreams can be achieved and you will either see them start to side with you or head in another direction. It will be a subtle change but it's coming, so look out for it.

It's not easy for some people to see others succeed because they are caught in the life trap too deeply and may never amount to much. It's your duty as their friend to help them to see the light but you can only do that through your actions and your success. My advice is to use their negativity and opinions towards you as rocket fuel for your success. Strive to show them that you are right and ultimately show them that if they just change their mindset they can do it themselves.

It's the most epic moment when someone tells you that they were wrong and that they are proud of you and what you have achieved. It's happened to me many times and I hope one day you experience the same.

Your success is coming for sure. The shift in mindset will open up doors and avenues for you. Sadly, you might lose a few friends in the process, but you will make many more also, and you will be happy that you found out people's true colours. Remember that success attracts success (I don't just mean financial success) and once you start becoming successful in life you will notice people are naturally attracted to you and you will have an incredible circle of friends and peers thanks to who you have become.

5. You will have to make short-term sacrifices for long-term gain

No one ever got anywhere in life without making a few small sacrifices. The main sacrifice will be TIME. But the sacrifices you have to make aren't necessarily big – you have already made a small sacrifice by taking the step to buying this book and reading it this far.

It's a case of doing two things:

1. Putting time into building your future
I discuss the time element later in this book as it's crucial to understand time. You will have to make some sacrifices where time is concerned because investing time is essential if you truly want to achieve your dreams.

Let me give you an example: If you watch only 1 hour of television a day that's roughly 30 hours a month. Do you think that time could be spent better? Of course you do. You've just created 30 hours every month you can dedicate to moving forward and achieving your goals.

Stop watching TV every evening and start building a business (or learning how – I can suggest many you can start from home today), start going to the gym, doing one of my online workouts at **TheBootCamper.com**, start a new skill, start a new course to gain another qualification... Spend that 30 hours a month doing something productive to move forward and it will have a huge effect on your future. You know it would, I know it would, but only you can make it actually happen. Don't delay!

Did you know that the average person in Britain watches 4 hours of TV a day... And the average American watches more than 5 hours of TV a day. Shocking statistic, isn't it? That's 150 hours a month and a whopping 1800 hours a year, which adds up to 75 days a year watching television.

It shocks me that people say they don't have time to change their lives, get healthy, start a business, learn a new skill etc. Come on! It's mind blowing when you hear people saying, 'I am too busy'. The average person is NOT too busy. It's easy to see that they have several hours a day free to do what they want, but they choose to sit in front of the TV. Madness.

Listen, I have two children that I look after full time as a single parent. I do everything for them yet I manage to also run my businesses, take the girls to their activities, put them to bed, feed them, do their washing, run the house and take them on days out etc. Trust me when I say

I know what busy is. But do I complain that I am 'too busy' to achieve results? Too busy to chase my ever growing dreams? Too busy to stay healthy and workout? No! I just get on with it. I do what's necessary in the time that I have available to me. My life is full on, but I love it and the fact is, we all have 24 hours!

I manage my time well. I work out what time I do have and break it into segments. Time for me to work, time for my children, time for my health and time to relax, and of course, time to sleep! The reality is that I work hard every day in everything I do because I know that every hour counts. It's not rocket science, it's just a case of realising that everyone is on a different journey and you are on yours. We all have the same 24 hours, it's just a case of fine tuning your time so that you can achieve the success you are looking for.

Let me give you another example: What if you were to go to bed just 1 hour later and wake up one hour earlier? Those two extra hours a day add up to an extra 30 days a year. You just gained an extra 30 days to build your future. Thank me later!

Please think about how you spend your time and how it will (positively or negatively) affect your future. and always remember that you will never get time back so choose very wisely how you SPEND it.

You spend money wisely because you've worked hard and earned it. So why wouldn't you spend time wisely too? You can work to get more money, so you can refill the money bank, but time isn't something that you can just work to get more of, you can't refill the time bank, you can't deposit more time. This means that time is a more important commodity than money. It's irreplaceable so spend it wisely. Spend those 24 units per day in the most productive way possible to achieve what you want out of your life. Don't waste it by spending countless hours a day watching TV, you will only regret it later in life. Don't say I didn't warn you!

2. Invest in your education whether that be time, money or both.
If you want to be the best version of yourself then you will need to be prepared to learn how to do this. You will need to make an investment into your education, either with your time or money or in most cases, both. This is crucial and shouldn't be ignored.

Buying this book was an investment in your future and for that I congratulate and thank you. It wasn't expensive and I could have given it to you for free, BUT there is a reason why I charge a small fee for this information and that's because statistically you are more likely to read it and action it if you have invested money in it. You have invested money into your future and you will get that back many times over by reading and applying what you discover in this book. I guarantee it.

By investing time in your future it will save you time in the long run. This book might be the first personal-development and success-education book you read, it might be your 100th, it doesn't matter. All that matters is that you are taking positive action towards developing your future and realising your dreams, rather than just being a drifter in the life trap like so many others. By investing time in yourself and this book you are learning the skills necessary to discover the exact steps you need to take to realise your goals and ambitions.

No one is an expert in all things, so my advice is to seek out the best person in the area you want to specialise in. Someone who is already living the life you want and study how they have done it. Put time, energy and, if necessary, money into learning how they got to where they are, and discover how you can do this for yourself. I'm not saying copy them as such, but just open your mind and discover how you can be the best at whatever it is you wish to become. Remember, success leaves clues and it can be reverse engineered. Do it.

4.

- You might not get a second chance -

Think about your life and what you are currently doing and answer these questions:

- **Are you truly happy?**
- **Are you currently where you thought you would be when you were growing up?**
- **Are you confident that you are on a path that you are destined to be on?**
- **Are you grateful for what you have achieved?**
- **Are you inspiring others with your success and making a difference in their lives?**
- **Are you doing what you love to do daily?**
- **Are you building a legacy that will outlive you once you pass?**

If you can't answer yes to all of these questions, take a long, hard look in the mirror and ask yourself, 'Why not?' What's stopping you? This life isn't a dress rehearsal!

From a young age we are all conditioned and educated to think in a certain way and live within a system that's been created for us. You know, go to school to learn how to be a good employee and then work your backside off for someone else for 40 years to eventually retire at 65 to finally be happy and 'free'. We are all taught this nonsense through our school systems. We are taught that life isn't all fun and games and that life isn't all about doing what you love, it's about working hard and climbing up the corporate ladder to retire and FINALLY be happy! Hmm.

What I have come to discover is that we are basically taught (read: conditioned) to work really hard in a job we probably won't like, to make money to live and pay bills. We are taught to conform to an exam system that is the same for everyone even though we are all vastly different. We are taught to be like robots. Why? We are not robots. We are not the same. We are all amazing individuals and we have different skills, different ways of thinking, different ideas about what we want to do in the future, different beliefs and faiths, yet we are all examined under the same system, which 'grades' us and makes us conform to achieve better 'success' in our future jobs because of a letter (grade) on our exam results papers. 'I got an "A" therefore I am better than you.' It doesn't make sense.

We are offered a whole range of subjects to study, many of which are simply not relevant anymore, yet we are still graded and categorised for our future based on the outcome of that result. It's the same at university but a little more fair due to the fact that you choose where you study and what you read. But it's a similar system nonetheless. (I went to university, but I don't do anything related to my degree now.)

We have been educated to believe that we have to conform to a certain way of life if we want to succeed. It's a myth, it's a trap. Don't fall for it. I'm telling you now to think for yourself. Think about your future, think about what you truly want to do, not what society tells you to do and certainly not what your exam results say you should be doing.

You owe it to yourself to think big and live your life your way.

I have dyslexia. My grades in my English GCSE (UK exams for 16-year-olds) were not great, I got a 'C', so that means I'm ranked relatively average in that subject. Yet here I am writing a book about how to be the best you can possibly be. I know many of my friends got 'A' grades yet they couldn't possibly write a book!

We had career talks at school and I vividly remember my English teacher telling me I wouldn't be an author. I also got a 'C' in business studies and my business studies teacher (who ironically had never run a business before) told me I would never run my own business. It's just not right. None of it makes sense. They are grading you on an old school system, literally. The modern world is very different so don't be put off from going after your dreams because of your school 'grades'.

Listen, I don't class myself as an author, but here I am, writing a book. So technically I am! I also run my own thriving businesses, many of which are literally changing people's lives.

If I had conformed to the conventional schooling system I would have been too scared to write this and I would have lived in fear of starting my own business because I am only a 'C' grade student. It could have stopped me living out my dreams – to help people worldwide to become the best they can be. Had I listened to 'the system' this would have literally stopped me from helping you right now.

This is wrong and certainly not the way it should be. I'm not an expert in the education of our youth and I'm not (for now anyway) going to start predicting or preaching about how it should be changed. But what I will say to you is that you have been conditioned.

You have been conditioned by a system that's designed to make you 'fit' into a system.

You have slotted right into the life trap but now you are learning how to get out of it. Well done you!

I got out of the life trap and I want you to do the same. The way I got out of it was through my car accident and by losing everything when my fiancée left me and the process I went through to become a full-time single dad. I don't want you to wait for a near-death experience or some horrendous personal circumstances to happen before discovering that there is a life trap, because you might not be as lucky as I was. You might not get a second chance in life.

We are all born. We all die. It's what you do with your life in between that time that matters. Your eyes have now been opened to the fact that you are in a trap. So now let's get you out of it so that you can absolutely smash life, be the best you can be and live a life of success, abundance, health and happiness. As I say, you might not get a second chance to live this life so let's make today and every day from here on in count.

Be the best you.

5.

- Don't wait until it's too late -

Let's assume that you live well into your old age. Let's say you live until you are 100 years old and you are lying on your deathbed looking back at this life you have lived. Let's go there. Imagine that's you now. Lying there about to die. A horrible thought it might be but bear with me as this is crucial to the next steps you take in life.

How do you want to feel when you're 100 years old looking back at your life?

- **Do you want to feel proud of the life that you have lived?**
- **Do you want to feel you have left something of value to the next generation?**
- **Do you want to feel that you have loved and been loved?**
- **Do you want to feel that you left a legacy for your children and your grandchildren?**
- **Do you want to feel that you were successful in all aspects of your life?**
- **Do you want to feel that you were compassionate towards others?**
- **Do you want to feel fulfilled and that your life wasn't wasted?**
- **Do you want to feel a sense of accomplishment?**
- **Do you want to feel that you have done enough and that you didn't miss out on anything?**

Of course you do. It would be the best feeling ever to die knowing you had fulfilled your ultimate life goals, dreams and ambitions. To die knowing that you had done yourself proud, that everything was complete and that you leave in true peace, happy in the knowledge that everything and everyone you left behind is better from your existence.

How would you feel if you didn't achieve any of it? Imagine if:

- **You didn't feel proud of the life that you have lived.**
- **You didn't feel that you left something of value to the next generation.**
- **You didn't feel that you had truly loved or had been loved.**
- **You didn't feel that you left a legacy for your children and grandchildren.**
- **You didn't feel that you were successful in all aspects of your life.**
- **You didn't feel that you were compassionate towards others.**
- **You didn't feel fulfilled and felt that your life was wasted.**
- **You didn't feel a sense of accomplishment.**
- **You didn't feel that you had done enough and that you missed out on so much.**

How would that make you feel? It would absolutely suck wouldn't it?

This is a very important lesson because, like it or not, one day it will be you. Literally you. Sorry but it's true. It's impossible to avoid because, without putting too fine a point on it, we will all die one day. I don't want to be too morbid here but, seriously, why aren't you making huge efforts towards living your dream life now?

I don't want any of us to ever feel bad or regret what we did or didn't do before we pass, it just wouldn't be right.

It must be the best feeling ever to pass in peace knowing everything is done and that you have left a legacy for your family and your loved ones. When I nearly died I would have left nothing, I wouldn't have achieved my goals and I certainly wouldn't have left a legacy. Don't let that be you.

Please don't go out still wanting more. Live a fulfilled life and enjoy every day, you owe it to yourself. We have one life and, yes, that's plenty of time, but you must always have the '100 year old' you in the back of your mind saying, 'I'm glad I did that', not, 'Damn I wish I'd had the confidence to do that.'

Don't live with regret. Embrace life. Live your life, your way. Be the best you.

Remember, this is all down to you, don't make the 'old you' regret the choices you make today. Be the best you and start today and make your older self proud when looking back.

Don't work your backside off for 40 years to make someone else rich with the dream of retiring one day to finally be happy, only to discover that you can't afford the life you wanted at the point when it's simply too late to change it. Do yourself a huge favour and don't fall for the life trap. You can easily write your own future, you literally have the pen and paper to map the whole thing out. Please don't avoid this lesson.

There is a book called The Top Five Regrets of The Dying by Bronnie Ware. Bronnie is an Australian nurse who spent a lot of time with elderly people in their last few months and years. I would like to share with you the top 5 regrets of the dying:

1. **I wish I'd had the courage to live a life true to myself, not the life others expected of me.**
2. **I wish I hadn't worked so hard.**
3. **I wish I'd had the courage to express my feelings.**
4. **I wish I had stayed in touch with my friends.**
5. **I wish that I had let myself be happier.**

Powerful stuff. I am sure you will agree.

Don't be another human being with a list of regrets in your final days. Be happy that you lived a life of compassion, love and success. Be proud of who you become and the legacy you will leave behind. All of this is yours for the taking.

6.

- Move past the past -

'I don't like looking back. I'm always constantly looking forward. I'm not the one to sort of sit and cry over spilt milk. I'm too busy looking for the next cow.'
– Gordon Ramsay

You can't move forward looking backwards. It's that simple.

If I was always thinking 'what if' then I would never move forward. I would always focus on the fact that I could have died and that I could be paralysed. But I am not, so I had to learn to move on, next.
Many people live in fear of change because of the question 'what if'. What if it doesn't work out? What if I look silly? What if I fail? What if...?

My answer to this is simple. What if it does work? What if you don't look silly? What if you succeed? What if you achieve your dreams?

I call it the 'what if syndrome' and I was diagnosed with it when I was recovering from my car accident. It's a little disease of the brain. It won't kill you but it will kill your future and certainly your success. It's a negative-thinking disease that stops you from moving forward and stops you from getting out of your comfort zone. You will notice it so much now I have brought it to your attention and you will even notice that you do it yourself, perhaps that you always have without even noticing (until now!). When you do catch yourself out, just notice that it's there, it's in your brain and it needs to be eradicated from your thoughts and vocabulary as soon as possible.

When I was recovering I had to see a counsellor about my anxiety. It was really bad. I kept dying in my dreams and I was very nervous about getting back into a car again especially as a passenger. I was in one of the sessions talking with her and she was asking me what the problem was, so I explained it all. She diagnosed me really fast and said, 'Do you know that you have said the phrase 'what if' at least 10 times now about things that didn't happen and won't ever happen?'

She was totally right. Part of my problem was that I kept saying things like, 'What if I had died? What if I was paralysed? What if the car had caught fire?' What if, what if, what if. I couldn't believe it. It was so obvious once she said it. It became apparent to me that she knew exactly what was wrong with me and via hypnotherapy courses my anxiety improved and I could finally look forward rather than backwards, worrying about things that never happened. It was a blessing.

The 'what if syndrome' was simple to cure. And here is how you can do it.

Firstly you have to let go of the past. What happened has happened, it's done and you can't change it and it certainly won't benefit you to waste time thinking about it. Every time you hear yourself saying 'what if' (and believe me you will be saying it) you have to spin it into a positive.

What if I don't succeed…? Becomes… What if I do succeed?

What if I fall…? Becomes… What if I fly?

What if I lose…? Becomes… Well, you get the idea…

What eventually happens is that you start to subconsciously think more positively. You start thinking about succeeding and about moving forward rather than backwards. By making a conscious effort to spin it around you will realise after a couple of weeks how much more positive you have become and how you have suddenly opened yourself up to a little more risk which, when striving for your success, can be a very good thing. You'll suddenly find that you want to give things a go. You'll find that you want to push to achieve more. You'll start thinking, 'What if this works out?' And you'll start to imagine the possibilities rather than thinking with a 'lack mentality'.

What you will also find is that you will start to think less about the past and think more towards the future. You will also, without a doubt, notice this 'what if syndrome' in so many of your friends and your family. Especially in the naysayers, which will enable you to understand their mentality more. They are so scared of the 'what ifs' that they don't try to better themselves and always assume that they will fail before they have even taken that first step.

Imagine the meeting at NASA for the first attempt to get to the moon. The conversation would go like this:

Start.

"I've had an idea, guys. Let's send the first man to the moon."

"But what if we fail?"

"Good point. Let's just concentrate on something else."

Finish.

It would just be ridiculous. So spend less time thinking about your past unless it moves you forward. Forget 'what ifs' because the past is done, it's happened, it can't be changed and will either work with or against you, so let's move on.

Successful people don't look backwards. They leverage the past for their own success moving forwards. Successful people learn from their mistakes and failures, and move forward knowing they've discovered another way not do something or learn a life lesson that will enable them to get the advantage next time.

You have to look at the past like that if you really want to move forward with your future. So many people look at what happened in their past as a lesson to their future but in a negative way. For example, I know people who have failed in business in a big way. They're very clever guys but because they failed once they gave up and quit, they got a job they didn't like and they miserably worked the 9–5 life and started living for the weekend again. They stepped right back into the life trap.

But as I said earlier, no one can ever really quit because time is a great healer and they soon realise that they still have the same burning desires and ambitions for success. However, the fact they are now back in the life trap means they have to go through the whole process again to get out. This means that many people simply don't bother and then make excuses to hide their bitterness towards their lack of success. Excuses like, 'I just want an easy life.'

In reality, what they are doing is looking at the past as an example of what could happen should they try again in the future. They make excuses like, 'What if I fail again'? So they just stay in that job, bitter and resentful towards those who go on to succeed when they don't.

They hate Mondays yet they justify it all by saying, 'I just want an easy life' or, 'The money is too good for me to turn down' and so on. How many times have you heard people say these things? The issue is that they are looking at past failures in a negative way, when in reality we know that failure is just research and is actually beneficial to their success journey.

Obviously we all want an easy life, but let me tell you now – doing something you love is way easier than doing something you hate every day. So what's the point in giving up on your dreams only to go and do something you hate pretending it's easier or because it makes you more money? Life becomes a chore and since when has a chore outweighed pleasure in the grand scheme of things?

If you have dreams, goals and ambitions (which you clearly have) you must follow them through and do everything you can to make them happen. Be relentless and never quit, even if that brings up some demons from past experiences and 'failures'. You must let it all go, move on and leverage your past experiences or you will end up living a life you truly hate and looking back with regret having accepted mediocrity.

The past is done. The future can be planned for but the NOW is all that really counts. Make the decision to change your future NOW and only take positive lessons from the past to move forward.

Remember, what if you succeed?!

7.

- Time is your best friend -

*'A man who dares waste one hour of time has
not discovered the value of life'*
– Charles Darwin

Time is our greatest commodity and something we will never get back. When it's gone, it's really gone so why waste it? Seriously, why?

You have to choose very wisely how you spend your time and who you spend it with. There are many 'time consumers' in the life trap to watch out for. For example: TV, video games, hangovers, newspapers, social media (Phone Zombies), a job you hate, a negative mindset and many more. They are out to get you and many have been designed to become addictive. They will sap time away from you and stop you from building the life of your dreams.

Remember what I said about wasted time watching TV? Well... Does it really matter who did what to who in a soap opera? No, it doesn't. Is it going to affect your future? No. It's not even real life!! I actually think soap operas create problems because those who are absorbed by them start thinking that real life should be the same as it is portrayed on the TV. The arguments, the affairs, all the drama. Life isn't and doesn't have to be anything like that.

What you choose to feed your brain isn't always the best food for your future.

Does it really matter if you complete that video game? Is the world going to end if you don't get to the next level? Nope. If you're a gamer, why not see your real life as a video game?

A real life video game where you have to do the best you can before it's game over? Start turning your real life into a passion and start enjoying it rather than being absorbed into another world, a fantasy world that doesn't really exist except in the form of code. Concentrate on making your real life better and building a future for yourself and your family. There are so many ways to monetise your passions to convert that to meaningful time that will enable you to build something tangible in the real world.

Does it really matter if you miss one news update from a friend on Facebook? No, it doesn't. There will be plenty more coming in the next few days, months and years so don't worry. You won't miss out.

None of this matters. Yet people consistently waste their time with it. WHY? Let's take television as an example. A bit of TV didn't hurt anyone in the short term. It's entertaining and of course I love some TV shows like the rest of us. But it's important to be selective when you watch TV and more importantly what you watch. Too many people have become addicted to TV and it's become an escape from everyday life and it's sad to see.

These 'time consumers' won't affect you in the short term but in this chapter you will discover how time, if used correctly, will always be your best friend. This will explain why the choices you make regarding where and how you spend your time will dramatically alter the outcome of your future.

Time, as far as we know, is infinite. But the time we have as human beings is not. It's actually, in the grand scheme of things, a blip in the existence of the universe.
As human beings we have a shelf life. The bodies we are

in get old and we die. Who knows what happens after that but all we know now is that we cease to exist in this form. This means we have a limited amount of time to achieve our dreams, our goals and our ambitions. We just don't have time to wait for 'something to turn up'. We have to take action and make it happen now.

So why is time our best friend? It's actually very simple. Once you learn how to use time as a tool you become a force to be reckoned with. Time ticks on every second of every day. What you choose to do with that time is up to you and it can either work for you or against you.

As I said before, time is more valuable than money. We will never get it back and we can never work hard to replenish it like we can with money and health (to some degree) so it's very important that we treat time carefully and as a powerful tool to get what we desire.

Time enables us to do many things, but it will never allow us to quit on our dreams because, as time ticks on, we realise that it is running out and the chances we have to achieve our goals and live the life we want get smaller by the day. So we then become keener and keener to fulfill our life goals.

We must use time as a tool to put our plans into practise and let them grow every day. It is called compound interest and once you master it, you will be able to build anything and achieve everything you desire.

Compound interest is all about putting in time every day, every week and every month towards your end goal. These daily actions compound over the days, weeks and years into the big result. If, for example, you want to lose weight, you need to eat healthier and exercise more every day. That's obvious, right? But that's not the whole story. There is another factor to weight loss and that is: Time. This is something most people don't realise. It takes time.

You see, everyone wants everything super fast these days but that's where they get it wrong. Time doesn't reward us with quick results if it's something worth working for. You could go on one run and eat healthier for a day and it won't make any difference at all. You could go on two runs and eat healthy for two days and you won't see any results. But if you do the exercise and eat better consistently for a couple of months you will start to notice a change in your body and in the way you look and feel. Our bodies are designed to adapt over time to whatever environment we put ourselves in.

The problem is that we live in a society where everything is so fast paced, where people want everything right now. But success and goals require determination, hard work and a solid plan of action executed over time to be achieved. Just as the farmer sows seeds to get the best harvest in the future, you have to sow the future seeds of success in your life starting with the first seeds now and then daily moving forward.

Compound interest requires you to put time and effort into achieving the desired end result every day. For example if you are putting in the time at the gym you are investing in your health. You have invested time (which is your best friend) and when you combine time with compound interest you will get the results you want.

Equally, if you do nothing, you won't achieve your desired results. By not exercising and eating badly, you may not immediately gain weight or become unhealthy but over a couple of months you will notice your health will have deteriorated and you would have gained weight. Compound interest works for you or against you but it never stands still because time doesn't ever stand still.

Most people don't know about compound interest so they wrongly assume that 'one more pizza won't hurt', 'one more cigarette', 'one more night out', and so on, won't hurt. Sure, it won't hurt initially but as time goes on and the rule of compound interest sets in you will notice that it's guaranteed to work against you.

By using time as a tool by leveraging compound interest you will find that you can achieve great results over time. Investing just 1 hour a day into your health is 30 hours a month. Which is an entire 15 days of the year. It soon adds up and you can start to see the power of this.

Let's look at it in a real-life scenario. If you wanted to learn to play a new musical instrument and you wanted to get up to a professional standard you can do it. You just need to find a teacher (or a mentor) and dedicate time each day and keep practising without fail. Over time you will get to where you want to be thanks to the power of compound interest.

Once you master this concept and learn that time works in your favour, you will see the results happen much faster than you thought. You need to start investing time into your education and start taking action by doing tasks towards meeting your goals every day and you will see the results manifest into your life.

The reality is that doing these daily tasks to reach your goals is actually very easy, but the problem for most people is that it's also very easy not to do them. Most people choose not to do the necessary daily tasks, without even understanding the rule of compound interest, and then wonder why nothing is happening for them.

It's exactly like the gym-membership craze that hits the first week of January every year. Everyone has a New Year's resolution to get fit and lose weight, so they join the gym. They buy the new gear, they go all in for the first week or two and then they think, 'This isn't working.' So they quit.

Why did it fail for them? Simple. It's because they didn't give it time. Time wasn't working for them, they were working for time. They went to the gym with high hopes that they would lose weight super fast and then the very next week they quit because they failed to achieve the unrealistic results they expected. It's ridiculous. If they knew how time could work for them, they would've stuck it out week by week, month by month, and they would've noticed the weight falling off and be proud and happy with their achievements.

Too many people expect results and success without putting in the time or the effort required, which is why the dropout rate at gyms is huge. 'This doesn't work' they say. 'Everyone else has good genes. 'Everyone else is lucky.' Sure, some people are lucky, but everyone and anyone can lose weight. The reality is that not everyone has the patience to do so. Or indeed the knowledge of compound interest to stick with it to see the actual results from their efforts. As I said before, time will never let you quit on your dreams so when people quit the gym they often do exactly the same thing again the following year! It's insanity. And what's the definition of insanity? Doing the same thing again and again and expecting a different result.

For me it's simple, put the work in daily and it's impossible not to see results. Remember, time is your friend, so spend it wisely.

8.

- Healthy body, healthy mind -

I started my health journey as a very overweight, depressed man and completely transformed my body. I know what the struggle is like. I am now a qualified personal trainer and I run a successful fitness business that I started from scratch. I believe that part of that success is due to the fact that I look at health in a different way to most people. I see the brain as 'you' and the body as a vehicle that you borrow for the duration of your life, however long that may be. I see them as two separate entities. Now that may sound weird, but let me explain.

By looking at it my way, it simply means that your body is the real home you live in. It houses all the essentials you need to potentially live a long and successful life. You need to exercise your body to be in the perfect condition for living a fulfilled life.

A healthy body gives you a healthy mind and that is a perfect combination for achieving your dreams. Yet so many people neglect their bodies. The brain is a separate entity and that's 'you', your consciousness, with the brain housing your desires and the ambition you need to succeed. But you have to give your brain the right tools for the job.

This isn't a book about weight loss, per se, but as a qualified personal trainer I have another book focussed on body transformations and nutrition plus an online workout platform so that you can train with me. We get serious results for our members, so head to TheBootCamper.com

You see, I used to be that guy who just didn't want to go to a gym, refused to do exercise or eat healthily – and boy do I love to eat! I saw exercise as a waste of valuable time that I couldn't afford to lose. Now I feel that exercise is a necessity that I have to make time for. I can't afford not to. It's a crucial part of my life! The method I am about to explain to you worked so well for me, and I'm sure if you follow this very simple concept you will have similar and hopefully better results.

Let me put it like this: If you are not doing a minimum of 30 minutes exercise at least 4–5 times a week then you are not being fair to your body. Your brain wants the success, the lifestyle and to live your dream, but you are not giving it the ability to do that because your body is out of shape and not running at peak performance. You are asking your body to give you the Ferrari of lifestyles but you are treating it like a beaten up old banger. It's just not right.

Your body is naturally doing everything it can to give you the best life you can possibly have so why are you abusing it? Do you constantly give it the wrong fuel? We are race engines, yet so many of us feed ourselves with low-grade fuel. We should be feeding ourselves with race fuel. Eating what we are designed to eat. That's how we give ourselves the best chance of success. How can you possibly achieve success if you are not pushing to get healthier?

Money isn't the only measurement for success and, as a personal trainer, I often say 'health is wealth'. Without putting too fine a point on it, what's the point in being the richest man in the graveyard? If you can't even be bothered to just get up and walk for 30 minutes a day, how do you expect to be on form and have the ability to reach your goals? Just 30 minutes a day (even 15 minutes to start with) is enough to get in better shape and to start releasing endorphins that make you feel happier, more energetic and more alive.

If you don't like gyms, don't join a gym. If you don't like sports, don't play sports. If you don't like running, don't run. But you MUST find something that you enjoy doing that exercises your body and your mind. Perhaps taking the dog for a walk would work for you, but instead of sitting on a park bench smoking a cigarette or being a Phone Zombie you should walk with your dog at a brisk pace.

The reality is that when you do something enough it will form a habit and you will start wanting to do that every day. I wanted to really make this work and see solid results so I could prove my concept to you before writing this book. For me, exercise used to be a real chore and I didn't enjoy it, so I wanted to test the theory I had about forming a positive habit and it really worked. When I started my body transformation journey I started by walking. Then I started walking and running in intervals. Now I've moved on from that and I train 4–5 times a week. Exercise has become a huge part of my life.

I am about to share a strategy that kick-started it all for me. I did this for about 4 months to start me off and, as I said, I now love exercise. I'm pleased to say that I'm in the best shape of my life. I'm not a bodybuilder (or even trying to be) but I can safely say at this moment in time I absolutely love exercising and I look forward to training every day.

Before you discover my strategy, I want to share my body transformation with you:

- This is my personal body transformation -

To discover how I was able to do this head to
TheBootCamper.com

So how can you do it? How can you create a habit and fall in love with exercise?

Firstly, you need to write down what you want to achieve and the timescales you wish to achieve those results in.

This is a very important rule with goal setting. You must always write down what you wish to accomplish. Personally, I wanted to start by losing 12 kgs in 6 months. That was my aim. A pretty achievable result you might think, but for me it was a very daunting concept.

I then needed to work out how I could do that with walking alone because I knew that I could stick to that in the beginning. It was pretty clear to me that I needed to leverage the power of compound interest and never give up. So I did exactly that.

I lost 12 kg in 3 months. Yep. It was incredible.

So how did I do it? I knew that if I concentrated on the weight and weighed myself on the scales all the time I would most likely want to give up, like I did in the past. Instead I threw away the scales and I tried a different strategy to form this positive habit in my life. I started collecting stones.

I know this is sounding weird but bear with me...

I picked a route that I wanted to do (with uphill and downhill sections) and I did it five days a week for 3 months without fail. I was living near the beach at the time, so I decided I would walk to the beach each of these days and pick up one stone and carry it back with me and put it in an empty jar. I did this consistently and not only did I end up with a growing pile of stones in a jar in my house but I had something physical, something tangible, to show for all my efforts.

If I had focussed on the weight loss alone I wouldn't have noticed the results of my exercising. But because I started filling this jar with stones I could literally count how many times I had been on my walk. It was real, it was there, my efforts were evident in a glass jar that was getting fuller by the day.

This went on for several months until it got to the point that I had completely filled the jar with stones. When I placed that first stone in the jar I made a promise to myself that I would fill it to the top. I thought it would take forever but once I had filled the jar, I weighed myself and the results were outstanding. I had achieved my goal, in fact, I had smashed my goal in half the time! But it was so much more than just losing the weight. I was now looking forward to the next walk, when in the beginning I was completely dreading it. The walks were getting easier, I was losing weight, I was losing inches around my waist, I was feeling better physically and mentally, I had more energy to play with my daughters and to be a better dad, I had more energy to work and I was less tired in the evenings.

The results were clear to see. Everyone complimented me on my weight loss and asked how I could have done it so fast. It was fantastic.

I realised that too many people chat about weight loss and put so much focus on the fact that they are overweight, that they convince themselves that it's hard to lose or that there is some secret to it. They weigh themselves every day and complain when they haven't lost a single pound! It's madness.

There is a secret to losing weight people just don't know about. It's a strategy and a system you need to follow and I recommend you try because you now know that it's persistence and compound interest that gets results over time. You must never give up.

When my relationship with my daughters mother broke up I became a full time single father. I decided to take my health and fitness very seriously. I went on to lose 36 kgs or 5.7 stone (which is 80 lbs). I completely transformed my body and I decided to qualify as a personal trainer to help others and I now run a successful fitness business. You can find out how I can help you to transform your body at TheBootCamper.com

I would recommend that you do a minimum of 30 minutes exercise 4-5 days a week. Just 30 minutes of walking or cycling, for example. You can do it before work, during your lunch break, after work, even multitask and sit on an exercise bike while watching a TV show or a movie, it doesn't matter really but make sure you do it, it'll change your life just like it has mine.

Remember this is a kick-starter, you're not training for a triathlon. This is an investment in yourself, an investment in your body that's doing all it can to help you achieve your goals. By committing to 4 or 5 days a week it will help you operate at your peak performance levels. It will change your mindset from thinking it's a chore to enjoying it and feeling amazing. You may find it helpful to do it with a friend or your partner or you could use it as a bit of time for yourself to enjoy some peace and quiet. Use this time to think about what you want to achieve in the day or during the week or listen to some music etc. Just remember to enjoy this time. It's your time and it's an investment in yourself.

If running is your thing then run, if walking is your thing then walk, if cycling is your thing then cycle, but make sure it's cardiovascular exercise that you are doing. If you want to lift weights then you can do that on top of the cardio, because it's super important we exercise our hearts as they are in fact a muscle too.

I personally recommend HIIT (High Intensity Interval Training) or circuit training and that's exactly what I do for my clients at my fitness boot camps and via my online platform no matter where you are in the world. It is the perfect blend of cardio and muscular endurance training and is the best way to transform your body. You can workout with me as your trainer with full support and a community that's got your back. We have created a growing library of 'follow along' workout videos for you.
Join us at: TheBootCamper.com

Obviously exercise needs to be complemented with a good diet. And again this is where people fail. They go on fad or juice diets, only eat meat, drop all carbs or follow a liquid detox diet. It's not sustainable (or healthy) and therefore it won't work long term.

There is too much to write in this book about healthy eating, so I wrote another book which you can access via my website TheBootCamper.com. It's called The Game Changer and it's a proven, sustainable way to eat to transform your body. I have had the most amazing results with my clients from this sustainable plan and I would love to hear your results with it.

I know this works, because it's exactly what I did to transform my body and keep the fat off! Get started now, you won't regret it...

9.

- Failure is research, not quitting -

'I have not failed. I've just found
10,000 ways that won't work'
– Thomas A. Edison

When pushing yourself to be the best and to achieve your dreams, you need to realise that you will fail. Potentially countless times. But that's not a bad thing and it's not something to be afraid of. In fact, if you change your mindset, you will see that it is a good thing. It's research. You are learning how to become successful with everything you do. And with failure comes perfection.

We all fail from an early age, but it's only modern society that has made us think it's a bad thing. Our conscious brain has made us think, 'What if I look silly?' or, 'What if I never make it?'. The 'what if syndrome' that we discussed earlier is working against you.

You should be proud of failure. That's the best way to look at it. You shouldn't care what others think about you because at least you have the guts and determination to work towards your dreams and ambitions. Most people don't.

When my children were learning to walk they would fail again and again. Get up, fall down, get up, fall down, get up, fall down. But did they then say, 'You know what, I'll just quit because I must look silly falling on my bum all the time. And crawling is a pretty decent way to get about so I'll just stick to that.'? Of course not. They kept going until they succeeded. They never gave up on their goals to walk until they were running around all day.

That was YOU once upon a time. That was ME and that was everyone in this world at some point. We all failed when we learnt to walk and continued to fail until we succeeded and started running, it was the same when we learnt to talk and when we learned to do pretty much anything. We are built to fail and try again until we succeed. That's how we learn. But for some reason as we grow up we start becoming fearful of failure. Why? I believe it's because we don't like to look silly and we have been conditioned to 'fit in' by doing as we're told so that we don't look or seem different to the others. My opinion is BE DIFFERENT. Be the best you.

I have failed countless times. Trying different businesses, different relationships, different jobs and on occasion it's made people say, 'What are you doing, Ben?' But you know what? I can safely say, 'At least I tried. I may have failed but now I know that's not how it's done, that wasn't the business for me, that wasn't the correct strategy moving forward, she wasn't the right girlfriend, that job sucked... But I learnt a lot that will continue to take me forward.'

That's the difference. I can see that failure isn't a bad thing. We try things and we learn from them if they don't work. The expression goes 'we learn from our mistakes' and we can also say 'we learn from our failures'. But for some reason the word 'failure' has a different meaning in society. Failure is a bad thing even though if you make a mistake it is acceptable if you apologise! It's a joke really. Making a mistake and failure are the same thing except failure has this stigma attached to it. Wipe that from your brain. Push forward being the best you, achieve your goals and don't get caught in this life trap.

Embrace failure, it's on your side. Go back to being that child you once were. You got up and tried to walk and even when you fell, you got back up – you were relentless until you got to where you wanted to be. Successful. Do the very same with your current goals and ambitions. Don't let anyone talk you out of it (even the naysayers). Fail and fail again until you smash it and you achieve your dreams. Even if that takes 1 year or 50 years, you have to go for it.

This is your only chance so don't let the fear of failure stop you. It's a myth, part of the life trap. Get out now and embrace moving forward. You owe it to yourself. You're doing this for yourself. And you will most likely inspire others on your journey and that is the best. That's the highest compliment of all.

'When we give ourselves permission to fail, we, at the same time, give ourselves permission to excel'
– Eloise Ristad

10.

- Stop looking for problems: Find solutions -

When was the last time you heard someone talk about a problem? Most likely today.

It seems to me that everyone talks about problems. It's like they crave having them. They actively look for problems to discuss with their friends and family, or even broadcast them over social media for the Phone Zombies to feed on. You know what I mean, problems at work, problems in their relationship, problems with their children, problems, problems, problems.

Most people discuss problems, but the fact is no one likes to be around people who just sit about complaining all the time. Often these serial complainers will find a problem in other people's success and view it as a yardstick with which to compare their own life. It's bonkers.

With the billions of people alive on this planet today, there will always be someone richer than you, there will always be someone fitter than you and there will always be someone who's the best at any given thing, but you don't need to look at them and judge yourself by their success as if it's a downfall in your own existence. Not at all. You need to leverage their success for your gain, be inspired and use it as a motivator to achieve your goals. You can model yourself on these people. I'm not talking about becoming a carbon copy of them, but success leaves clues, so discover how they got to where they are and use that research to help you on your journey.

If you want to be the best at something then who better to study than the best in the world? But most people don't. They find problems and feel inferior because they haven't achieved certain levels of success. They see friends they went to school with driving a better car than them, living in a better house, working in a better job and they get jealous or insecure. They see it as a bad thing, they judge their own lives based on the success of others, which is totally the wrong way of looking at it.

You need to congratulate that friend because through their hard work and persistence they have achieved what they wanted to. Chances are they might not be where they see themselves ultimately, but because you assume that they have 'made it' you see that as a reflection of your lifestyle and how badly you are doing, and for some reason that hurts you. This is insanity. My advice would be to reach out to them and offer to buy them a coffee and chat about the good old times and see if you can get some advice about moving your life forward.

You can't judge yourself by the success of others. We all have different circumstances, different DNA and ultimately different journeys. We think differently, we act differently and we are all gifted in our own ways.

Sadly people will always find problems and something to moan about. It drives me mad. From the weather to their health to even jealous traits about why someone is thinner than them or why other people have better material possessions. This is not healthy.

You need to find solutions and leverage other people's success to help move your own life forward. If you have successful people in your area, get to know them. Don't be resentful and push them away. Most people have a desire to share their stories with others, much like I have done in this book. So it's better to embrace their success and learn from them than to push them away and spend your time with an unsuccessful peer group who aren't going anywhere. Remember, success leaves clues and you never know, they might be able to open some doors for you.

I'm not saying if you have friends who are unsuccessful you have to ditch them, but as soon as they are talking negatively or talking about problems just try to change the conversation to a more positive tone. It's contagious. You will notice that over time they will slowly change to be more positive. If they don't then you have three choices, you can tell them straight by saying, 'You're very negative and you really need to start looking at the brighter side of life', or you can reduce the time you spend with them and limit it to be dependent on the conversation, or you can just cut them out completely. The third option is hard and might not be an option for you but, as I said before, time is not infinite for us so you have to choose how you spend it. Remember if you spend a lot of time concentrating on people's problems and not moving forward with your success, the compound interest effect will start working against you.

Spend time with people who inspire you, not with those who hold you back and discourage you from seeking an efficient route forward. Go out and fix the problems. Don't spend your life dwelling on them because, as Henry Ford said, 'Whether you think you can or you cannot, you are right.' There are billions of people in the world who have problems and most of their problems will be a lot worse than yours. It's not the size of the problems, it's how you overcome them.

11.

- Be the best you -

'Do your best when no one is looking. If you do that, then you can be successful in anything that you put your mind to'
– Bob Cousy

You have to be the best you. You just have to. You owe it to yourself, to the people in your life and those you engage with both directly and indirectly. It's so important. By being the best you, you will get a lot further in life. Don't put your future success at risk by getting sucked into the life trap. Be yourself and make it the best version of yourself. Don't be lazy, don't take the easy route, because it won't create your future how you want it. Do the work, put in the time, put in the effort and you will see the results. I guarantee it. You need to start NOW.

So the next step is a small task for you.

I want you to write down your goals and ambitions. Write them down in detail. Not on your computer or your phone. Go old school and grab a pen and paper and write the following:

Where do I want to be in 1 year from now?
I will be...

Where do I want to be in 5 years from now?
I will be...

Where do I want to be in 15 years from now?
I will be...

Where do I want to be when I retire?
I will be...

What do I want to have achieved when I look back at my life from my deathbed?

I will have achieved...

This step is very important. Go into as much detail as you can. Take a couple of hours out of your day, maybe take the weekend to think about it and then write it down in detail.

For example, write down things such as where you want to be living, what car you want to be driving, how many children you want, what you want your family to be doing when the kids are older, who you want to hang out with, where you want to go on holidays, where you want to retire to, what you want to have achieved when you look back from your deathbed and you could even write down what legacy you want to leave when you pass.

This is all very powerful and by writing it down you are planting that seed. I did this during my recovery to get my brain thinking forward not backwards. Many of the things I wrote down have become my reality already and the others are certainly becoming more real by the day, such as writing this book with the aim to help and inspire over a million people. This book has been in my mind for many years and I'm so grateful and excited to finally be writing it. The thing is, you have to know what you want before you can get it.

You don't just get in the car and drive anywhere hoping you end up at the destination you want, do you? You get in the car with a clear knowledge of where you want to end up. You have a road map of your journey, and in many cases you have a satnav telling you where to go.

Let this list of your goals and ambitions be your life's satnav. Let this be the guide to your future success. You can make your life anything you want it to be. You can be as successful or as unsuccessful as you want to be. The choice is all yours, but remember: Life's for living and you get out of it what you put into it, so enjoy creating the road map and planning out your future.

Once you have written down the details of your future you will need to photocopy it twice and keep the original somewhere safe. Put the first copy in your wallet or purse where it needs to stay. You should take this out every now and then to remind yourself of what you want to achieve and to keep yourself on track. Put the second copy in your bedside table and read it as often as you can before you go to sleep and when you wake up. By making sure you have it on your person and by reading it often it will stop you falling back into the life trap.

You can look at this list in the years to come to see how far you've progressed and what areas of your life you need to improve on. Some things will need more effort than others, so just keep on track, stay focussed and make the positive steps forward every day. Remember, time is our best friend.

Your goals and ambitions are one thing but they're not the only thing you need to work on to be the best you. You need to be the best you can be in all aspects of your life. This world is full of people who are drifting through in the life trap. Don't be another victim. You will need to do some specific things to get out of the trap. They are simple strategies but you will get so much more out of your life by applying them to your lifestyle immediately.

1. Be a good person

You know what's right and wrong. Most people do, but the world we live in is messed up for the most part. People are generally good and I believe we are born into this world with good intentions. But some people are drifting through life on the wrong path and they don't realise what they are doing. It's not necessarily their fault, they just haven't woken up to it yet and many won't, but that's their choice. Most people are conforming to how society says they should be and they can't see past that. They live week by week, complaining and moaning, finding problems and being negative. That's up to them. You can help but it's only your actions that will enable them to see the error of their ways. Let your actions do the talking.

I believe the reason for this is that society has made most people scared. It's made people assume that everyone is a bad person and a threat. This isn't actually the case at all. Yes there are some bad eggs out there but I find that 99% of the people I meet are actually really good people. But it's as if they are scared to be themselves and they feel that they have to conform because they don't want to act differently to their peers or be their true selves because that's too much of a risk. They wouldn't want to appear to be 'too out there' because what if they aren't accepted or what if they look silly? Who cares? It's your life, you have to be you.

Most people are scared of not fitting in or being rejected, as if acceptance is the most important thing. Most people who have found success have done so because they had the guts to stand out and make themselves leave the pack to achieve greatness.

You need to do the same. Be a good person. Be the best person you can possibly be. Snap out of your current state. Start being the best, stand out, be a leader. Do it now.

Being a good person will open so many doors for you. Being polite and courteous, being generous, being respectful, holding doors open for others, saying hello to people you meet, smiling, being kind, it all costs you nothing but can get you very far in life. This is something that's becoming completely lost in our world but needs to be brought back.

Please. You owe it to yourself, you owe it to your future.

2. Be yourself
You have to be yourself. You are incredible. The fact that you are reading this book tells me that you already have what it takes to achieve greatness, but you will only do that by being yourself.

You also have to be true to yourself. Be true to who you really are. That's essential if you want to really succeed. You can't lie to yourself about who you are; just accept the real you and embrace it.

Too many people try to conform and change themselves to fit into society's ideals. Don't do it. You don't need to. You know who you are but chances are that you do things in your life just for the approval of others because you don't want to be an outcast, right? You won't be. And if your peers can't accept you for who you truly are then why waste your time with them? Take action, be true to yourself and you will be free to move forward with your life. If you are pretending to be someone you're not or changing yourself to fit in then you're holding yourself back big time. You can't live a lie.

Ever since my accident, I changed. I changed to be who I truly am and many people noticed this. My friends and family noticed it big time. I just wasn't the same person anymore, not just in my physical appearance but in the way I acted, in my opinions and my philosophies on life.

I spent a long time researching who we are, why we are here and why I didn't die in that car accident. It was eye opening for me and I've become a much better person because of it.

I didn't find the answers in religion. I didn't find the answers in science. I found the answers inside myself. I had to be me. I had to be true to myself and start living my life, pushing for my goals and my ambitions, helping others, and being the best person I could be. I'm improving every day on this and it's getting me so much further in life.

Physically, I look totally different now. I'm in decent shape and I'm really into my health and fitness. I had laser eye surgery so I didn't have to wear glasses anymore, I grew a big beard because previously I felt that I couldn't for fear of not being able to get clients and not being accepted as I wouldn't look 'smart' at business meetings. I changed my dress sense and I decided to just be who I really am, who I wanted to be. And you know what? It's from the moment that I accepted to live my life how I wanted to that things really started changing for me.

Since I made that decision everything changed. You need to do the same. You have to be yourself if you are going to be the best version of you.

3. Smile

Look around you at the general population. They don't smile. You'd be lucky if you even got a smile from someone on the street. We're human beings, we are all the same, yet we are not interacting on the most basic level. A smile. That is sad isn't it?

Human interaction at a basic level seems to be a character trait that becomes lost as we get older. My kids smile at everyone. They don't have this fear people seem to have about smiling or making eye contact with people. My kids will see people as we're walking along and they will smile at them and many people don't even smile back, it's weird. When I smile at people I get a lot of strange looks, but why? This is a basic human interaction at a grassroots level. Maybe I'm the weirdo?! But a smile can make someone else's day. You don't know that person's situation. They could be having their own issues and by smiling you could have brightened their day. It cost you nothing, it took up no time but that smile could be worth a million bucks to that person.

Yet we don't do it enough. Most people walk around with their head dipped staring at the floor and looking miserable, when their whole temperament and attitude would change if they just looked up, held their head high and smiled confidently. Try it, you will like it. And when you get a smile back from someone, it's a great feeling. It's like a mini, friendly conversation with that person. You may even feel very daring and say 'hello' or strike up the basics of conversation with them like, 'Nice day, isn't it?'. Often that will snap people out of their pattern and also brighten their day. It's a good place to be and I recommend it.

There will be those who think you are bonkers. But let them think that, you have done your bit to be nicer. It's a good thing.

4. Talk to people

Every day is a networking event. You never know who you will meet. Everyone has a story to tell and a lesson to share.

When I was backpacking around the world I discovered that it's so easy to strike up a conversation with people. And more often than not it's eye opening to hear other people's stories even if it's just a short glimpse into their life.

If you are standing next to someone in a queue you can fire up a conversation. It's easy to do and 90% of the time I find that people want to chat. They are bored, either being a Phone Zombie or just staring into space. I'm not necessarily talking about a long conversation with everyone you meet – remember you have to choose who to spend your time with – but the person you are standing next to in a queue could be literally anyone. I find that fate often puts people in our lives for a reason, and some of the people I have met randomly have become good friends, clients and great contacts for the future.

I find that the elderly love a quick chat. I get the impression that once you get to a certain age it's like you become a ghost and you are basically ignored. The world must be moving so fast around the elderly with modern technology, mobile phones and a text-chat culture – it must be a very strange place if you grew up in the days of writing letters and having 'normal' conversations. So if I'm standing in a queue or waiting for a train to arrive, I tend to strike up a conversation instead of wasting that time. It's incredible who you meet and it's wonderful when you make someone's day because they are lonely and someone has made the effort to speak to them. That person could have been exactly like you when they were your age or perhaps they are the same age and on a similar journey to you and you could work together to both move forward. You could meet clients, business partners, investors, new friends, find out new stories, find out tips and advice – you never know.

I've met many clients for various businesses I have run from randomly striking up conversations and chatting. For example, the neurosurgeon who was helping me when I broke my neck became a client of mine when I was running a web design business. We got chatting and he asked what I did and then he became a client. As I said before, fate can sometimes put people together for a reason.

I want to tell you a quick story about why I like to talk to people at every opportunity... A few years ago I sat down in a cafe with my double espresso and I was sitting next to this old man who I would guess was in his early 90s. I wish I could tell you his name. I struck up a conversation in my usual style because I hate sitting near people and just staring into space like he was.

So I said, 'How's your coffee? It's good here isn't it?'

He looked shocked that someone had made the effort talk to him.

'What was that?' He said.

'Oh, sorry to disturb you. I was just asking how your coffee was.'

'Too hot!' He said, which made me laugh. 'It's good though. Why do you ask?'

'Because it's good in here,' I said.

'You know, I've come here for years and you are the first person other than the staff to even acknowledge me,' he continued.

This hit me hard. It was shocking. How could he have been here for years and not spoken to anyone? He said something to me then that I will never forget. 'The youth of today just have their heads in their phones. It's a real shame they are missing so much of life.'
This was powerful to hear from someone at the tail end of his life talking about the youth of today. We got chatting and he had some incredible stories. We chatted for 45 minutes and the conversation was totally one sided. He never found out what I did or anything about me. In fact, he never even asked, but that didn't matter because what happened next changed my mentality about people forever.

We got chatting about his life. This was not your average old man. He had been in World War Two as a young man and we were discussing how the world had changed and it really opened my mind. He had some really sad stories about how he had lost friends and loved ones in the war – it was clearly still emotional for him to talk about.

He almost cried. He said he was so lonely and that this world had become so fast paced and so different than what he was used to. He said that he missed the old days and was grateful that I had spoken with him. He said it's a rare thing because a real conversation is something of the past and it's all texting and 'that thing called Facebook' now. Everyone has their heads buried in their phones and don't even speak to their family most the time. I told him I called them 'Phone Zombies' and he laughed in agreement.

He said he felt very lonely in his old age. His wife had passed away last year and he had his daughter and granddaughter who lived up north and they only came to see him a couple of times a year. They were shopping at this time so he decided to sit and have a coffee. We laughed as we would both rather be relaxing over a coffee than shopping.

He then said, 'Can I let you in on a secret?'

'Of course' I said.

'I have terminal cancer and I have just come out of the hospital where I had a check up. I don't see the point in these check ups as I'm going to die anyway but my daughter insisted I went. I haven't got long to live now the doctor said.'

I was stunned. What the heck should I say to that? The old man had been chatting to me for nearly an hour and now he's dropped this bombshell on me. I had just found out all about his past and now I had discovered he was about to pass away.

Suddenly his daughter and granddaughter came back with their shopping bags. They sat down and within a matter of seconds they were both silent, face down on their mobile phones being Phone Zombies. He looked at me and I could see sadness in his eyes.

Then he turned and said to me, 'You've made my bloody day.'

Then he sat in silence for the next 10 minutes almost in tears while his daughter and granddaughter sat next to the oldest member of their family, in his dying days, face down on their phones ignoring him. I was shocked and, for once in my life, speechless.

Please remember this story and be a good human being. Strike up conversations with people. You never know what lessons you will learn or how you will affect their lives.

R.I.P old man from the cafe. You left a legacy, a message and I'm sharing it for you now.

5. Follow your passions

You have to do things you love in this life. Life's for living, they say. So live it. Stop doing things you hate. If you hate your job then start looking for better options. There is nothing wrong with a job, don't let the 'business gurus' or anyone else tell you otherwise. I have plenty of friends who are killing it in their jobs and loving every moment. But it's important that you don't look back with regret having spent 45 years of your life in a job you hate working for someone else.

Look for alternatives. Look for jobs you would love to do with a real career ladder to climb. Jobs where, as you improve, you get paid more for the effort and time you put in. We all have to make money but you don't have to spend time doing something you hate, feeling trapped by your boss, being stuck in the life trap as well as the rat race. There are other options. For example, you could relocate to find a job within an industry you love if there aren't any in your home town. You may need to take a lower wage but you will be happier and you can then work up the ladder within that career path.

If you need to get extra qualifications to get the other job, do it. I ran various businesses for many years but when I became a full-time single dad I had to do something around my commitment to my daughters. I decided to get a diploma in personal training. I invested in my education and I got another qualification to further my career. I love it and I now get to call my passion my work and I am truly blessed to be in the position to help so many people in the process.

My advice is that if there is a job (or if you can create a business) where you can work on your passions every day, do everything you can to make it happen. Even if that means further qualifications. That time invested in your education now will bring you years of happiness in your future. I am living proof of this fact.

If you want to start your own business but need the income and couldn't afford to quit your job then you can get a lot done between 8 p.m. and 2 a.m., and on the weekends. Especially if you normally go out every weekend spending your money on partying! You could use that money and time to start investing in your education and in your own business.

Think about your future. Don't do a dead-end job you hate. Start actively looking for something you love, or at least enjoy (whether that's another job or working for yourself), because the opportunities to grow will be there, you just need to take that leap.

Working for someone else doing something you hate really isn't a good long-term plan. Don't leave immediately, educate yourself and take positive action towards changing your career direction, to follow your passions. I have changed my career path many times, failed many times, but now I can happily say I am on the perfect path for me and I'm loving every second of it. Let's make that happen for you.

6. Enjoy life and enjoy the journey

Make the most of life. Enjoy every day as much as you can. Live every day as if it's your last.

You don't know how long you have on this planet. I don't know how long I have left but because I nearly died I have a completely different view on this second life I have been blessed with. I want you to look at things differently after reading this book.

Please leverage my experiences for your gain and understand that life's a journey that must be enjoyed. Life can be taken away so fast!

Your life journey is unique to you and it can go in any direction you choose but it's important that you enjoy it. Of course there will be sad times, you might even lose loved ones and have tragic things happen. But try your hardest to see the positive in every situation and you will really start to see the real joy of life.
Losers find a problem to every solution, winners find a solution to every problem.

It all starts with you. No one else is going to enable you to enjoy your life, but your enjoyment and passion for life will be contagious and will rub off on others.

It's not looking back at your life that's the exciting bit. It's the journey of life that's to be enjoyed, every day with the future goal of looking back feeling proud of what you managed to achieve.

That journey of achievement starts now, so start enjoying it and making it the best journey you could ever wish for. Make it your reality.

12.

- Start now -

'It always seems impossible, until it's done'
– Nelson Mandela

What are you waiting for? Your future is right in front of you. Get out of the life trap and start moving forwards and taking action to create your perfect life. Don't wait for the perfect time to start. It may not present itself and that's because there is no perfect time. Start now.

Don't wait for perfection. Forget ready, aim, fire. You need to work with: READY – FIRE – then AIM.

Get started now and then fine-tune to perfection later. Just get started and take action towards the life of your dreams. Start now.

The only person standing in the way of your success is you. Become a success story, become a somebody and make something of your life.

Leave a legacy and leave this planet in the knowledge that your existence was worth something. Leave knowing that what you did counted. Leave knowing that your family is proud of your achievements and that you left something of value for their future.

What are you waiting for?

You now have a road map to get started. Start living your life. Get healthier, get wealthier and be happier. Be the best you and get out of the life trap before it's too late.

- Connect with me -

INSTAGRAM: Instagram.com/benhulme

FACEBOOK: Facebook.com/benhulmeofficial

FINAL WORDS:

Thank you to everyone who has supported me since my accident. There are too many people to mention here but I am grateful to every single one of you especially my family and friends.

Thank you from the bottom of my heart for reading my book. I am beyond grateful.

It's been a really tough journey to get to where I am now, having gone through my accident, to my depression to losing everything I worked for and becoming a full time single Dad but I can safely say I am a better man for it.

I have learned and grown as a person from everything that's happened to me where many would have curled up and simply quit.

This book has been created in my head over the past few years and I am so happy that I now get to share it with the world with the aim of inspiring and motivating others.

I really can't wait to hear about your success and I hope that this book has been a catalyst to get you started on the next part of your journey.

Sincerely,

Ben Hulme
BenHulme.com
TheBootCamper.com